The Ferguson Story

Beginnings

After various attempts to fit his linkage to other machines including the Fordson, Ferguson set about building his own tractor, which was assembled at his May Street, Belfast premises in 1933. Many components were bought in and castings in light alloy from Short's foundry were used. A Hercules engine, David Brown gearbox, and Ferguson three point linkage, resulted in a 16 cwt. machine as opposed to the 30 cwt. of the Fordson.

The Ferguson draft control which was applied to the tractor gave added adhesion when using the Ferguson implements designed specifically for the tractor. It was claimed that there need be no problem as regards the weight of the tractor, except, of course, when you towed anything behind.

Unit construction was applied and the prototype had this split into four components; engine, clutch housing, gearbox, and rear axle were flanged to each other. The clutch was a single plate unit, and a three speed constant mesh gearbox took the drive to a spiral bevel rear axle, which in design was similar to a lorry rear axle, but with the front cover flange being mated to the rear of the gearbox housing.

Independant brakes were fitted to assist turning, and the tractor was mounted on spoked type wheels similar to those on the early Fordsons. It could be operated on petrol or kerosine, but the manifold design did not allow for very efficient vaporisation of fuel oils. Ferguson preferred petrol as a tractor fuel anyway!

With a prototype, looking very much like a reduced Fordson, in existence, Ferguson then set about getting the tractor into production. David Brown of Huddersfield had supplied some components for the Black tractor and following negotiations, agreement was reached whereby David Brown Tractors Ltd., a new company, would build the tractors and Ferguson would take care of the selling.

The first type 'A' tractors were ready by May 1936, and the design of the Black tractor was followed closely. The clutch and gearbox housing were now combined, and a Coventry Climax L head engine of 3.125" bore and 4" stroke was now used. This side valve unit ran at 2000rpm and gave 20HP. It featured pressure lubrication and shell bearings which details were a distinct advantage over the Fordson engine. Unlike some units built by Climax themselves, a self starter and water pump were absent, on cost grounds. Magneto Ignition by BTH was used.

The colour of the tractor was changed to battleship grey. Ferguson wanted production models to be black but his staff persuaded him to change.

The location of the hydraulic pump however did create one nuisance in that the hydraulics would only operate when the tractor was on the move and in gear. One had to be on the move when raising the implement and this could be very awkward at headlands when ploughing.

After the first 500 tractors the Coventry Climax concern was retooling for a new engine, so David Brown bought the patterns and built the final 800 or so engines themselves.

Four implements were available initially, a 10" two furrow plough, a ridger, and spring or rigid tine cultivators. A single furrow 12" plough came later.

Allied to its own equipment the tractor performed slowly by modern standards but did the job - the engine lacked the guts needed for even two furrow ploughing. Its main shortcomings could be allied to bad manifold design which was later corrected, but not by David Brown, as several proprietory makes of Vaporisers were put on the market. Another weakness was the use of alloy castings. Some steel transmission housings were actually cast and some even fitted. This increased the weight of the tractor by about 3cwt. At least one tractor had a PTO fitted, a feature which production tractors lacked.

In the two year period of production David Brown Tractors learnt a lot about the shortcomings of the original design and tried to persuade Harry Ferguson to allow them to build a more powerful tractor; this Ferguson resisted. The two concerns parted company and David Brown started building their own VAK1 model from 1939. Although three point linkage was available on the David Brown tractor, it lacked the draft control of the Ferguson which was protected by patents.

The Hand

The demonst... rry Ferguson at Hen... he famous 'Handsha...

The agreemen... ...ors and Ferguson to market... ...s organisation.

With the benefit... ...developments in automotive engineering, t... ...n team, along with Ferguson's men Sands & Greer, ...ed the real forerunner of the modern tractor. To speed production use of standard components was encouraged, and apart from the Ferguson Hydraulic System the tractor showed its Ford parentage very well in the use of an engine which was half a Mercury V8, and transmission and other components common with other contemporary Ford products.

Prototypes were to hand in March 1939, and by June production models were available for demonstration. The tractor was very much in line with contemporary Ford styling, and the four cylinder side valve engine of 3.125" bore by 3.75" stroke developed 24HP at a maximum speed of 2200rpm. The engine was machined on the same line as the V8 units, an extra shift being put on to cope with the extra production.

Just how much Ferguson's team influenced the design is subject to question, as Ford design policy very much revolved round the 'team' idea, and Ferguson's three men just became - pro tem - part of that team. Certainly the hydraulic linkage was pure Ferguson, but the incorporation of the hydraulic pump into a square transmission housing and driven from the PTO seems to have originated with Sorensen. The beam type front axle was the brainchild of Sands and Greer. Ferguson himself would have liked to have seen an overhead valve engine fitted to the tractor, but the costs of development and timescale for planned production ruled this out

The selling organisation which was set up also included the brothers Sherman, who had sold Ferguson ploughs earlier on, and the new selling Corporation was in part financed by a loan of $50,000 from Henry Ford.

The tractor was an instant success and put behind it all the weaknesses of the type 'A'.

There was, however, nothing in the agreement in the USA to allow for production of the Ford 9N in the United Kingdom. Ford of Britain were virtually independant of the parent US concern in 1939. Attempts were made to get 9N production started in the UK, but Percival Perry, head of Ford in Britain, found himself drawn into some rather unfortunate politics concerning Henry Ford.

Ford, who was recovering from the after effects of a stroke, was not in full command of the situation, and the attempts by him to force Dagenham to produce the 9N caused a rift between Perry and himself. In any case the matter was in fact outside Perry's hands, as the War in Europe had effectively placed tractor production under Government control and there was no way the Government would allow a break in production to happen.

The 9N did reach the United Kingdom; fitted with modified Holley 295 Vaporiser to run on TVO and designated the 9NAN. Ford in the UK handled all spares and service on these units imported under lease-lend.

Wartime shortages caused a utility model to be produced, on steel wheels, and without battery reliant electrics or self starter. The 2NAN was the UK equivalent of this model. Edzel Ford, Henry Ford's oldest son, who had a hand in styling the 9N, died in 1943. This left a gap in the Ford empire filled by Henry Ford II in 1945.

The new chairman had the onerous task of putting the Ford operation back into the black after the ravages of war, and his attitude to the production of a tractor sold by another organisation was hostile. Henry Ford II realised that the bad business judgement of his father had created the problem, indeed a simple agreement in writing might well have overcome many of the later unpleasantries, therefore the sales agreement was terminated in 1947. The relationship between Ferguson and Ford had sadly deteriorated, not helped by wartime shortages and the end result was that by 1948 Ford were building their own tractor, the 8N, which was simply an improved 9N, and selling it through their own sales organisation.

The new Ford tractor had a four speed rather than a three speed gearbox and improved hydraulics with means of overriding the Ferguson draft control. By this time of course the TE-20 was being built in England, a tractor of very similar design to the 8N.

The termination of the agreement naturally left a 'no supply' situation in America, and Harry Ferguson was forced to import such tractors as he could from England. He therefore filed a complaint against the Ford Motor Company on 8th January, 1948, regarding the use of the Patents held by him with regard to the hydraulic system on the Ford tractor.

The trial started on 29th March, 1951. The sum of $240,000,000 was claimed as a result of the introduction of the Ford 8N and the consequent loss in business to the Ferguson organisation, and the unlicenced use of the Ferguson system, which was patented, on the new Ford tractor.

After long and costly proceedings, Ferguson accepted a settlement of $9,250,000. This was only to cover the unauthorised use of the Ferguson hydraulic system, the claim against loss of business was dismissed.

The Ford Motor Company were instructed to stop production of the Dearborn or 8N tractor by 1952, but the Ferguson Patents had already been extended and were soon to be out of date. Ford's new 1951 model the NAA had a fully 'live' hydraulic system with engine driven hydraulic pump and its introduction necessitated the updating of the then current TO-20 model in due course. Most modern tractors now have the draft control pioneered by Harry Ferguson, usually with the Ford innovation of the over riding feature which allows the lift to be used under 'position control'. This latter feature was not approved by Ferguson, yet from the 35 on it became standard on all M-F models. In due course manufacturers such as Ford and M-F often came to reciprocal agreements over the use of each other's patents. So complex had the situation become over these that M-F and other makers set up their own patents departments run by Lawyers to ensure that any new ideas they had were covered, and also to make sure that in building anything new they were not in infingement of anybody else's patented designs.

During the war, some 2N tractors had been supplied to the US forces for airfield and other uses, without the Ferguson system, and to complete the story illustrations of these are included in this book.

The TE-20

Ask any Ford salesman of the late forties and early fifties what he feared most and he would tell you "The Grey Menace". Such was the success of the product of a new relationship between Harry Ferguson and the Standard Motor Co. which provided the Irishman with a tractor which, for the first time, challenged the supremacy of Ford in the United Kingdom.

Following the failure of getting 9N production started in the UK, and the breakdown of the 'Handshake Agreement' in the USA, Harry Ferguson was left without a tractor to sell in the United Kingdom. It was fortunate that a surplus capacity in the automotive industry was evident by 1945; having ceased military work many of the motor manufacturers were looking for ways to use the 'shadow factories' of the war years.

Such a plant existed at Banner Lane in Coventry and, approached by Harry Ferguson, Sir John Black of the Standard Motor Company was receptive of the idea of building tractors there, indeed it was hoped that the whole range of Ferguson Implements could also be produced. With continued Government restrictions, there would be problems in obtaining the correct tooling and materials.

At the time Standard were about to develop a new engine for the new postwar family saloon car - which became the Vanguard on its appearance in July 1947. This could be adapted to fit the tractor, but in order to get production started engines had to be obtained from elsewhere.

There was a great need in postwar years to earn dollars and as the new tractor would primarily be for Eastern Hemisphere sale this created difficulties with the Ministry of Supply. Licences had to be obtained to import anything and permits had to be obtained to allow purchase of any materials, from a washer to a complete machine tool.

An approach to Sir Stafford Cripps, Chancellor of the Exchequer in Britain's new Labour Government, was made by Harry Ferguson, and suitably impressed at the possibility of bringing work to war torn Coventry, arranged sanctions for machine tools and raw materials. There was a twist to this however, as the permit for engine imports was only to last until as long as it took to get the new engine into production at Coventry. Now by getting the funds to develop a new engine, ostensibly for the tractor, the same engine was also to be used in the new car. Some clever bargaining by Sir John Black with the Ministry of Transport ensured that the engine was sanctioned and it was phased into tractor production in 1948. As the new car was a potential dollar earner, and 60% of production was to be for export, the first engines actually went into the cars, their export in effect countering the import of the 'Continental Z-120' engines. Early advertising for the Vanguard car even played on the fact that alternative engines were being economically produced for both _cars and tractors.

As for the tractor itself, it was simply an updated 9N with four speed gearbox, and the benefit of an overhead valve engine. Ferguson had managed to obtain a full set of drawings for the 9N during early production and it was on these that the new tractor was based.

While problems in the Western Hemisphere were involving Harry Ferguson, production at Banner Lane built up satisfactorily, and in due course the tractors became 100% Standard engined.

There was of course one disadvantage with the Ferguson System, and that one required the proper implements to use with the tractor for it to reach its full potential. Unfortunately the idea of these being built at Coventry soon evaporated, and it was from a multitude of engineering firms and machinery suppliers that the tools for the three point linkage came. At least with the other makes of tractor which were designed for trailed implements some adaptation of horse drawn tackle could be made as a stopgap, but not with the Ferguson. Its weight distribution did not make it suitable for hauling certain types of implement.

The second problem was that the tractor ran on Petrol. Now, in theory, petrol was still rationed in 1946; indeed it was 1950 before all restrictions on its use were lifted. Enough fuel could be obtained in the usual way for agricultural use, but it was subject to excise duty, whereas TVO was not.

Harry Ferguson was initially against a low cost fuel variant, but as the home market gradually opened up it became necessary to add the TED-20 to the range. This required an engine with a lower compression ratio and suitable vaporiser. Indeed once the TVO model had been established, a zero octane (lamp oil) model was also offered for export from 1950.

The Petrol engine developed 28.4hp at the belt and was of 80mm bore and 92mm stroke. Now the car version of the engine was, after initial development, set at 85mm. Again Ferguson was not keen to increase the power output of the tractor. He was want to point out that it defeated the object of the exercise.

The TVO model was only rated at 26hp at the belt, and it was pointed out that by using the larger bore engine the power could be increased to that of the petrol version. This was agreed, but when the change to the 85mm engine took place on 22nd January, 1951, at serial 172501, the larger engine was fitted to all spark ignition models.

With the competition fitting diesels in production, it was not long before Ferguson's sales force were calling for a diesel version of the TE-20. Now as Harry Ferguson himself was not a diesel fan, it took some considerable persuasion to get him to agree to a diesel engined tractor at all.

Although the source of the Petrol and TVO engines for the TE-20 tractors built in the Eastern Hemisphere was of course the same Standard Motor Company, Ferguson was under no obligation to buy engines from that concern. At the time of development the only really suitable engine available was the Perkins P3, and this was still under development. Perkins offered the P4, but but it was a rather expensive item, (as was the P3), and developed too much power in the eyes of Harry Ferguson. Freeman Sanders became involved in the design work on the diesel engine which was commissioned initially by Ferguson. Part of the deal was that development costs would be shared equally if the same engine could be adapted for use in the Vanguard car. In the end H.F. had to bear all the development costs, as by the time the car went diesel, Massey Harris had become involved on the tractor side.

The resultant unit was dry linered, and had a bore and stroke of 3-3/16" x 4", indirect injection layout, chain driven camshaft and fuel injection pump, and turned out some 2Cwt heavier and 1.25" longer than the petrol unit. This meant that it was not conceivable to provide units to convert previous production tractors to diesel, as the build of the TEF-20 as it was designated on its introduction in June 1951 had to take dimensional variations into account. Kigass equipment was provided to aid starting, but even with this feature the engine had a reputation for sluggish starting in cold weather. A single heater plug was situated in the inlet manifold. Strange to say, when the engine was finally fitted in the Vanguard car in 1955 separate heater plugs for each cylinder were provided - some engines of this type did eventually get into a few tractors.

The only effect that this had on other models was the adaptation of 12 volt electrics for all models from the 250001st tractor in 1952. This was in any case only following the trend in general for 12 volt systems in the whole motor industry.

In addition to the standard tractor, demand grew for narrower versions once the potential of use in vineyards and orchards was realised. The factory built narrow version came out in 1946. This lost 6" in width by fitment of narrower axle shafts. In 1952 the Vineyard model became a factory assembled option and by the use of smaller tyres a reduction in overall height of 2" was achieved in addition to a reduced width of 32" minimum track.

The diesel model was never offered in Narrow or Vineyard form in TE-20 days, although conversions were offered by Reekie Engineering, Jack Oldings, etc. These firms had started by converting standard spark ignition tractors, indeed some Ford/Ferguson 9Ns were also dealt with.

By the early fifties tractors were also becoming more used in industry, and a whole range of allied equipment was advertised for use with the Ferguson, from mobile compressors to a complete drive on roller. A pleathora of variations were offered for industrial use, from basic tractors to those with full front and rear fenders, extra braking, and lighting, to comply with the Road Traffic Acts.

Everybody thought that the TE-20 would go on for ever, but already, as we have seen, the model had been effectively superseded in the Western Hemisphere. Over half a million Grey Fergies were built from 1946-56, at the time the largest production run of any tractor in the UK.

Developments in the Western Hemisphere

The end of the relationship between Henry Ford and Harry Ferguson almost put paid to the US market as far as Ferguson was concerned. The production capacity of Ford, now that they had ceased to supply Ferguson, and launched the new 8N Dearborn tractor complete with its range of implements, would build some 442000 plus units from 1947-52. This tractor was based on the 9N but had an extra speed, and improved hydraulics, and was built from July 1947.

In the meantime, Ferguson had acquired a small plant near Detroit, and in October 1948 production of the TO-20 (tractor overseas) was started. This was very similar to the TE-20 and used the same Continental Z-120 engine. Naturally sub-assemblies and electrical components came from U. S. suppliers. A number of TE-20 tractors were imported from 1947, and this is one of the reasons why, sdespite the Standard engine being used in U.K. production from 1947, tractors built at Coventry used the Continental Z-120 engine until July 1948. Some 60000 TO-20 tractors were built up to August 1951. In the same period Ford built and sold 7 times the number of 8N tractors!

The tractor market in the USA postwar was far more competitive than that in the UK in postwar years. Although the Lawsuit with Ford's had the effect of causing the production of the 8N to be stopped, Ford's were ready for this and launched a new model in late 1952, the NAA. Ferguson was ready for this in the USA, and launched the TO-30 from August 1951. This used the larger Continental Z-129 engine which had a 3.25" bore and 3.875" stroke. Hydraulics were improved The "Scotch Yoke Piston" type pump worked at up to 2300 psi. on all US built Ferguson TO-20s and 30s. Continental remained the main source for engines in the Detroit built tractors until the diesel and Perkins took over in the late fifties.

In 1954 the TO-35 was introduced. The Z134 Continental engine now had a bore stretched to 3 5/16". Like all U.S. built Ferguson tractors to date it retained six volt electrics, but had a redesigned gearbox with six forward speeds, and an improved four piston hydraulic pump. Position control was introduced to the hydraulics; this was done as Ford models from 1948 had been thus equipped, and despite this facility effectively 'locking out' the Ferguson draft control by now HF was only a part of the Massey Harris Ferguson concern, and market demands, in the Western Hemisphere at least, held sway. The TO-35 retained the TO-20 appearance, but was finished in a green and grey colour scheme in deference to the then Ford colours of red and grey. A diesel version, using imported Standard 23C engines, was also offered.

From 1958 the two line policy was phased out and the two models were abandoned in favour of a revised Massey Ferguson 50 finished in red and metallic grey, but with styling more in keeping with the Massey-Harris precursor. In addition the Perkins 3 cylinder 3A-152 diesel was fitted into this machine. The Massey Ferguson 65 Dieselmatic introduced at the same time in the USA used the Perkins 4 cylinder 4A-203 engine, and had almost identical styling. From 1960 the 65 diesel sold in the USA became identical with its Eastern Hemisphere counterpart, and in due course this received the improved, direct injection Perkins AD4.203 engine. The MF35 diesel also adopted the Perkins 3A-152 engine.

In addition to normal models the M-H-F 202 and Massey

Ferguson 202 and 204 were offered in the USA. These models were for industrial and commercial use and featured optional power steering. The 204 had a 'Reverse-O-Matic' transmission consisting of a flywheel mounted torque convertor, plus hydraulically activated forward and reverse multiple disc clutches, giving pedal operated instant forward and reverse.

The end of the two line policy in the USA also meant the virtual end of the Massey Harris lineage as far as tractors were concerned. Armed with the new Perkins engine facility at Peterborough the trend was towards diesel power in all models.

The first new model to appear was the MF 85 in 1959. This was available with a Continental 242 cu. in. gasoline engine, the same engine adapted to run on LPG, or a Continental 276.5 cu. in. diesel. This model was renamed the 88 in 1960. In 1961 the Super 90 Diesel replaced the 88, and this had either Continental Gasoline/LPG engines or a Perkins A4.300 diesel. This latter engine was the first specifically built at Peterborough for tractor use, and all mountings were cast into the cylinder block, rather than being bolted on. The A4.300 had a bore and stroke of 4.5 x 4.75" and developed 61/68HP @ 2000rpm. The Super 90 was built until 1965.

One final line of development needs to be looked at before moving on. Massey Harris had a presence in France where 'Pony' tractors had been assembled from early postwar years. It was the French plant which was chosen to build the MF25; called a replacement for the TE-20 in some quarters. This tractor had a Perkins 4.107 diesel of 3.125" bore and 3.5" stroke which gave 20/24HP @ 2000rpm. This model was imported into the USA, but not into the UK. The prototype of this model was in fact a Fergie 20 fitted with a Perkins 4.99 engine; the 4.107 being a bored out version of the latter.

Post Merger Developments

A more powerful version of the TO-20, as the equivalent model was called in the USA, actually came in August 1951 with the fitting of a larger Continental Z-129 unit, but unlike the English equivalent, the model was redesignated the TO-30.

It was in 1954 that the TO-35 with even larger bore in its engine came onto the Western Hemisphere market. This tractor also featured a six speed gearbox and improved hyraulics, with position control fitted. Production at Ferguson's Dearborn plant never reached that of Banner Lane, in fact by the end of the TE-20 in 1956 Coventry had built 517651 units and Dearborn only 169000.

Now under Massey Harris control, in effect, although the merger of 1953 was an effective takeover in real terms, it was 1956 before a new model came in the United Kingdom. The TO35 came onto a market where a 'two line' policy was operated in the Western Hemisphere, with Massey Harris models continuing in production for sale through former Massey dealers, and Ferguson for sale through Ferguson dealers.

It so happened, that after the merger, Massey Harris dealers in the USA, mainly due to the unpopularity of the then current M-H range, asked for a Masseyised Fergie.

The result was the Massey Harris 50, which was simply a Ferguson TO-35 altered to provide a rowcrop beam style front axle, which could also be replaced by a single front wheel or vee twin wheels, increased ground clearance, and provided with Massey Harris style tinwork.

There was a resultant backlash from the Fergie dealers in the USA to this model, and the Ferguson 40 was created in 1956. The tractor was 'deMasseyised' with distinctive new tinwork and sold through the Ferguson dealers.

The 'two line' dealer policy was phased out in 1957 and the need for two different models subsided.

By fitting the Perkins 4.192 engine to the Massey Harris 50 carcass the Massey Ferguson Dieselmatic 65 was introduced in the USA. Frontal styling was 'halfway' between Ferguson and M-H tradition. In fact, apart from the improved gearbox there was little more to this machine than the Ford Ferguson 9NAN into which Frank Perkins fitted a P4 for his own use during the War. It took another ten years or so for the power to be applied to basically the same transmission.

To provide the UK with a similar tractor, the press tools for the 40 tinwork were shipped to the Banner Lane plant, and thus the 65 in Britain took on the appearance of the erstwhile Ferguson 40, with important differences.

Double reduction hubs were provided at the end of the axle shafts and disc brakes fitted.

Later 65s received the Perkins AD4.203 engine which was now direct injection and developed 58.38hp @ 2000 rpm. The original engine put out 50.5hp.

A final feature of late series 35 and 65 tractors was 'Multipower'. This doubled the number of working speeds. A hydraulically operated high/low range with on the move shift capability was fitted ahead of the main transmission train. A separate hydraulic pump, mounted on top of the main tractor hydraulic pump in the rear transmission, provided the power source. One design flaw was that engine braking was not available in low range - a weakness which the author of this book found to his cost on one occasion.

Industrial models of both the 35 and 65 were produced, and these had the option of torque convertor transmission. The 35 was also produced in Vineyard form, with a diesel engine avilable on this model for the first time.

After the merger, in the United Kingdom, where dealer structures were somewhat different, many Massey Harris dealers found themselves selling Ferguson tractors after 1954. You had the situation where some dealers sold Fordson tractors and Massey Harris implements - there were not that many M-H tractors sold in the UK anyway! Changes in the Ford policy regarding dealers, with a move away from their car and truck dealers selling tractors unknowingly helped some dealers to change to 'grey'.

The late 1956 introduction of the FE-35 brought this new model onto the UK market later than anticipated. Unlike its US counterpart, the TO-35 the tractor featured revised styling, and instead of a tilting bonnet it had a service flap to gain access to the fuel tank(s).

The TVO and Petrol engines were now of 87mm bore and were rated at 30/34hp. The diesel had the new 23C engine which now had a bore of 84.14mm and was rated at 37hp @ 2000rpm. In due course a dual clutch and 'live' PTO were optional.

Finished in a grey and gold colour scheme the new model looked very smart, but the diesel version soon gained a reputation for being a bad starter; Harry Ricardo had been brought in to improve the engine and it seemed that the 'improvements' had a detrimental effect!

The Massey Ferguson hierarchy were none too happy that the Banner Lane plant was not in their ownership. Protracted negotiations started in 1957 to take over the plant; this did not involve the engine production facility.

It so happened around that time that F. Perkins Ltd., of Peterborough were passing through less fortunate times. The onslaught of 'own make' diesels, coupled with the success of Ford's new 590E and 592E engines, plus the drying up of the conversion pack market was taking its toll on sales. Still a family concern in effect, Massey Ferguson had the opportunity of obtaining capacity to supply diesel engines for both Eastern and Western Hemisphere operations on acquisition of the plant. Until that time, US tractors had used Continental Diesels.

By 1958/9, both Banner Lane and the Peterborough plant of F. Perkins were under MF control. Faced with a drying up of sales for its engines, the Standard Motor Co. even considered building its own tractors; indeed prototypes were even built. The planned range of implements and the tractor never came to anything - New Idea were to be involved but in the end Standard had to be content in selling its 23C engines to Allis Chalmers for the ED40. They continued to supply petrol engines to MF, and also to Ford for their Dexta.

Perkins had successfully updated their P3 engine for Ford to be used in the Dexta, and at the same time took the opportunity of revising their own production unit. The result was the P3/144, a development of which very soon found its way into the Ferguson 35 as the P3/152.

Gone were the cold starting problems associated with the 23C engine and the 35 settled down to a successful run which lasted until it was superseded by the 135 in 1965. During that time further improvements were made. 'Live' Hydraulics and PTO also made their appearance, and from 1962 the 35X with more powerful Perkins A3/152 engine was introduced. Even after Perkins came under M-F control, engines were still supplied to Ford for both the Dexta, Super Dexta, and other applications; indeed other tractor manufacturers as well still fitted Perkins.

We now have to go back in time to discuss the introduction of a larger tractor of totally new transmission design, not allied to the 20/35 concept as the 65 was. It is well known that Harry Ferguson was opposed to large tractors, yet by 1950 he was beginning to realise that the only way into the growing world market was to build a bigger machine.

The experimental and design departments at Fletchamstead, Coventry, in anticipation of the forthcoming merger with Massey Harris, began work on a larger tractor, and some six prototypes were assembled between 1952 and 1956.

The engine was designed by Polish Engineer Alec Senkowski and was so arranged that it could have 2,3,4 or 6 cylinders and could be built for petrol, diesel, or TVO operation. About a dozen engine blocks were cast; it is not known how many were built up. Most of the extant photographs show a tractor with a petrol en-

gine designated the 45C. If volume production had been attained the tractor would have been designated the TE-60. After it was realised that the '45' engines would prove very expensive to produce, a Perkins L4 was tried in one of the tractors. The original TE-20 design showed weaknesses in the rear axle which were never overcome. The LTX used a double reduction rear axle design to reduce the load on the crown wheel and differential.

Once Massey Harris had a hand in the affair, the larger end of the market, was, in effect, covered by the 744 and 745 models. But as we have seen elsewhere these were not doing too well as far as sales were concerned.

The cost of putting the LTX into production was prohibitive, so Massey Ferguson, as it became in due course, looked elsewhere for a means of bringing a tractor to compete with the Fordson Major, Nuffield Universal Four, and International BWD6 onto the UK market.

The scene was now set to provide the basis for the next generation of tractors, apart from the fact that the French MF plant, inherited through Massey Harris, launched their own small tractor in 1963. The 25, this tractor had been developed using a four cylinder Perkins 4.99 engine in a Fergie 20, the final model receiving the slightly larger 4.107 engine. This tractor was also known as the 30 and the 825 during its short production run. One unusual feature of this model was the location of the hydraulic pump in the top housing of the transmission.

New Designs for the Sixties - the 100 Series.

By the early sixties, it can now be seen that there was a certain amount of standardisation in the MF tractors built in both Eastern and Western Hemispheres, unlike Fords, for example, whose designs in England and the USA were totally different.

With the trend towards unified product lines moving ahead in all automotive fields, MF took the step to introduce a completely new range of models in 1965, with unified styling and specifications worldwide. The demand for Gasoline engines was still evident in the USA, and thus Continental engines still appeared in these tractors.

The MF135 replaced the 35, the MF150 the MF50 (available only in the Western hemisphere), and the 165 the 65. In fact these models bore a similar relationship to each other as the 35-50-65 did. The use of Perkins engines saw the MF135 and MF150 fitted with the AD3.152 engine, the MF165 had the AD4.203 of its predecessor. Whilst Continental engines were still available in all these models, the Z134 in the 135 Special, the Z145 in the MF135 deluxe, and MF150, and the G176 in the MF165, Petrol versions of the Perkins engines were developed and the later MF135/MF150 became available with the Perkins AG3.152 engine and the 165 with the AG4.212. Six forward speeds were provided in all models along with two reverse, but the equipping of any model with "Multipower" doubled those. The 135 retained the beam type front axle of its predecessor, whilst the other models had the usual arrangement to allow the use of row crop type equipment. All models had a new styling with "squared up" appearance.

The 175 was a new model, and featured a Perkins 4.236 engine. This was designed specially to fit the tractor, and was the first Perkins engine to feature the inlet and exhaust manifolds on the same side. Indeed, when the 165 was updated in 1968, the old style AD4.203 engine had given way to a new unit based on the 4.236 but with shorter stroke, the 4.212. The American built 180 was similar but designed for rowcrop work.

Hydraulics on all models except the 130 were improved, with the addition of 'pressure control' which allowed draft control to be used with trailing implements. One feature of all models apart from the 130 was the use of many common transmission components.

In 1971 the 175 was replaced by the 178 with a larger engine, the Perkins A4.248.

In November 1971, in time for the Smithfield Show, the 100 series was expanded to cover six models. These consisted of the three models of the basic range, which could be purchased in 'Standard Rig', with no Multipower, manual steering, live PTO, etc. often to suit export markets. The 135 and 165 continued as before, whilst the 178 had been replaced by the 185 earlier in the same year. The basic range were very price competitive for those customers who did not want too much sophistication. The above did not feature gearbox spacers.

The first cabs made available for the 100 series were not safety cabs, indeed they were constructed of fibreglass. The first safety cabs were of composite construction with canvas (plastic) infill, and the option of engine side shrouds which diverted engine heat to warm the cab. From 1971 the option of a rigid clad type cab was available at extra cost. In due course full safety cabs to 'Q' specification had to be supplied for UK use, but as the 100 series were being produced mainly for overseas markets by the mid seventies, it was often the case that domestic sales received proprietary cabs.

One of the problems when a cab was fitted was the restricted access to the driving position. This was overcome by introducing a spacer on the 100 series 'Super Spec' tractors from late 1971, which fitted between the gearbox and rear axle and lengthened the wheelbase of the tractor. This allowed the fitting of a more spacious safety cab. It also altered the weight distribution of the tractor to advantage, allowing the attachment and use of heavier implements without the need for front weights. With these improvements, including the use of spacers, the 135 became the 148, the 165 became the 168, the 135 the 148, and a stretched version of the 185, the 188 was also introduced, in time for Smithfield Show in 1971, where the improved range were shown. The 'Super-Spec' tractors also had independent PTO, Multipower transmission, spring suspension seat, high capacity hydraulic pump, and in the case of the 188 only, power steering and power adjusted wheel track.

In practice the range of models was complicated by the fact that if a customer desired he could up-grade a basic model or down grade a 'Super-spec' model. Where Multi-Power was not specified a new eight speed gearbox was offered on all models except the 135 and 165 which still used a six speed unit.

But the spacer idea was also put to good use in using the space for an optional 'creeper' gearbox in place of the spacer. As far as normal gearboxes were concerned, the 130 had an eight speed gearbox within high and low ratios, whilst the other models had a basic six speed transmission over high and low ratios, which became 12 with the application of 'Multipower', which was optional.

The smallest model sold in the UK was the 130, which was an update of the MF30 built in France, with a Perkins 4.107 four cylinder diesel. On the other hand, the largest conventional tractor available on world markets was the US built 1100, fitted with the Perkins A6.354 diesel or a Waukesha F320-G six cylinder petrol engine. This became the 1130 when fitted with a turbocharged version of the diesel engine, the Perkins AT6.354. The 1080 was a relative, but this had a Perkins 4.318 diesel; this tractor was derived from the US built 180 and was also assembled in France. The ultimate in 100 series power was the 1150 built at the Detroit plant from 1970-72, which featured a Perkins V8.510 diesel. At the other end of the scale, the French plant specialised in the Vineyard (Vigneron) and Orchard (Etroit) models based on the 130 and 135 tractors. By using derated and uprated engines 122, 140 and 145 models were offered, the 122 Vigneron having a 4.99 rather than the 4.107 engine of the 130, and the 140 and 145 engines used the 3.152 engine set to run at 2150 rpm and 2250 rpm respectively rather than the standard 2000 rpm.

The black tractor built in Belfast in 1933 is seen above and right. A Hercules engine was fitted.

Top: The type 'A' was often used with equipment for which it was not suitable - the horse rake shown here would however be within the capacity of the tractor.

Right: A sole prototype with cast iron transmission case and PTO was built. The PTO position is seen here - the tractor is preserved.

Below and Bottom: A Vineyard version of the type 'A' was produced and this had a set back front axle to allow for greater manoeuvrability in confined orchards and groves.

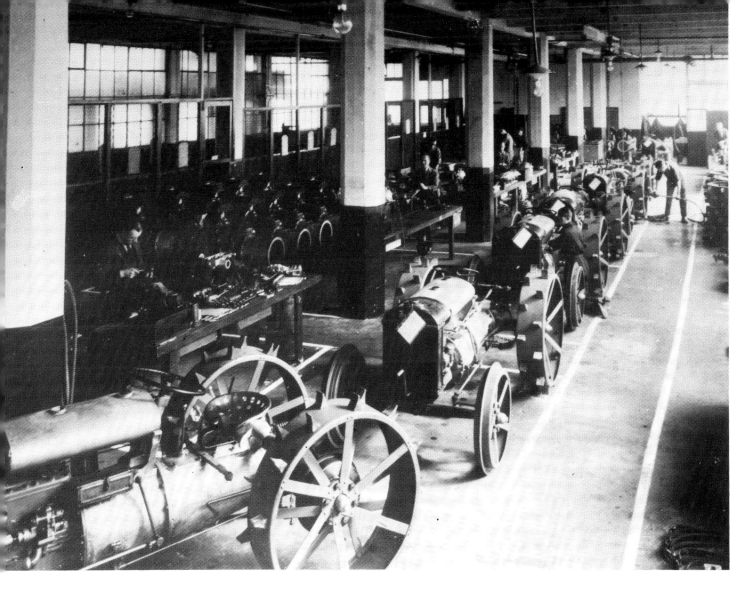

Above: Finished tractors come off the line at David Brown's Park Works at Huddersfield. Production was on the flow line principle, although with a total of 1200 type 'A' tractors being built, it could not be described as mass production. At the same time Fords were building around ten times the number of units in one year!

Below: Implements were also assembled at Huddersfield, this view shows ploughs and toolbars in various stages of build-up.

Above: Henry Ford & Harry Ferguson with the type 'A' he took to Fairlane for demonstration.

Below: The prototype 9N with rather austere styling. (Henry Ford Museum).

Above and below: The final production tractor was developed in less than a year.   Here Harry Ferguson and Henry Ford pose with one of the early production tractors, and a Dearborn built plough.

Above: 9Ns roll off the production line at Dearborn. This tractor is being fuelled up ready to be driven away.

Below: Some of the team involved with the development of the '9N'. They are left to right; Harry Ferguson, Henry Ford, Edsel Ford, Charles Sorensen, George B. Sherman, J. L. Williams, and Eber C. Sherman.

Above: The New York World's Fair provided the opportunity to demonstrate the 9N to the public for the first time. Here Harry Ferguson and Edsel Ford watch the president of the Fair, Mr. Grover Whalen.

Below: At the American launch of the Ford Tractor with Ferguson System on 29th June, 1939, Henry Ford is seen being admired by a small boy.....

Above: He then handed the tractor over to this small boy, who ably operated the tractor in the demonstration area.

Another early tractor with a young operator is seen in the field below. The rowcrop capability of the 9N can be seen (right) with the wheels on this tractor set at the maximum width of 76".

Above: 9N tractors were turned out for use by the US forces in the War. Here are two 'militarised' versions with cabs, fenders, and lighting equipment. Around the time that these were being supplied, Edsel Ford was attempting to persuade his father to withdraw from the US tractor market altogether, as Ford Motor Co. were losing a lot of money on supplying 9N's to Ferguson. (Henry Ford Museum).

Below: From 1942 on, the Ford 9N received a vertical bar grille, more of contemporary Ford styling. Although the two tractors shown here appear to have full electrical equipment, the 2N model was launched with no self starter, a magneto, and steel wheels in most cases instead of rubber tyres. (Henry Ford Museum).

Above: This shot, taken at the Greenmount, County Antrim, Northern Ireland, in October 1939 shows one of the first two tractors shipped to Northern Ireland, or indeed the United Kingdom. It was used as a demonstrator whilst the other went to McGregor Greer of Tullylagan who backed the project financially. Note the steel rear wheels, not common until the wartime shortages produced a starter and battery-less model 2N.

Below: Ford marked the break with Ferguson by introducing an improved model, the 8N, which had an extra forward speed, improved hydraulics, and other detail differences. Fords built and sold some 442000 of these tractors from 1947-52. Later 8N engines dispensed with the front mounted distributor in favour of a gear driven unit of more conventional design.

Opposite Page Top: The 9N after its 1942 grille restyle.
Centre: The 9NAN with Holley vaporiser was supplied under lease-lend to the United Kingdom to allow low cost TVO fuel to be used.
Bottom: Finished in Olive Drab, and fitted with bumpers, subframes, and grass tyres, these Ford 2N's were about to go into military service when photographed in 1943. They were supplied, less hydraulics, to the military direct, a procedure which did not help the by then somewhat strained relationship between Ford & Ferguson. (Henry Ford Museum).

The Ferguson TE-20 closely resembled the Ford Ferguson 9N. Easy identification of tractors assembled in the U.K. with Continental engines can be made by noting the kink in the exhaust after it leaves the manifold.

The original Fergie 20 is seen here with a two furrow plough The Continental Z-120 engines had to be specially imported and import licenses obtained; the use of a UK built engine as soon as available became a priority.

Harry Ferguson's publicity stunts often smacked of the bizarre. he staged his postwar press conference at Claridges' to launch the TE-20 onto world markets, and proceeded to drive it across the ballroom, and then to the consternation of hotel staff, through the crowded lobby and out into the street. The tractor is an early TEA-20 with Standard 80mm engine. Careful preparation ensured that the tractor was 'dry' - there was no oil in the sump in case of leakage, and only a cupful of petrol was put in the tank. Even so, the engine was dismantled later in the experimental dept. at Fletchampstead, Coventry, and no ill effects were found.

Tony Lees, Public Relations Manager and Harry Osborne, Advertising Manager for Harry Ferguson Ltd., look on as the Fergie 20 is driven out of Claridges into the street.

Above and Below: The TEA-20 with Standard engine - similar to that fitted to the Standard Vanguard car had a successful 8 year run.   Various modifications were made over that period.   The engine was bored out to 85mm from 22nd January 1951, and 12 volt electrics were fitted from tractor 200,001.

The TED-20 (V.O.) and TEH-20 (lamp oil) models were introduced from 1949, and can be easily identified by the manifold shield.

Above: The Ferguson TED-20 was the most popular model with UK farmers until the diesel engine was developed.   The inevitable problems occurred when the tractor was used on light work when running on TVO however.

Below: Tractor 200,000 comes off the line at Banner Lane.   This was in theory the last of the six volt tractors, it would appear that some were still to come! Harry Ferguson is in the driving seat with Sir John Black alongside, whilst Alan Botwood looks on.

The narrow version of the TE 20 catered for situations where it proved impossible to use a normal width tractor. A TEC-20 (petrol) model is seen here, whilst TEE-20 (V.O.) and TEJ-20 (Lamp oil) models were also available, the latter being introduced in April 1950. Track width was 42" instead of the 48" of the standard model.

Introduced in April 1952, the Vineyard model closed a gap in the sales area which had been covered by dealers doing their own conversions. A TEL-20 (V.O.) model is seen here with wheels set at the normal track of 32". The same model is seen below with track set out to the width of a normal tractor.

Above: A comparison of the rear of the Vineyard model with track set fully out, and at the normal 32" setting.

Below: The reduced height of the Vineyard model is seen when compared with a normal width tractor.

A vineyard tractor at work.

Above and below: The Diesel engined TEF-20. The engine was longer and could not be fitted to existing Ferguson tractors. The clutch housing was also different as the starter was on the RH. side of the engine. Note the location of the batteries and the chief identification feature, the pre cleaner below the exhaust manifold.

Right: The diesel engine installation. The unit was developed in conjunction with Freeman Sanders.

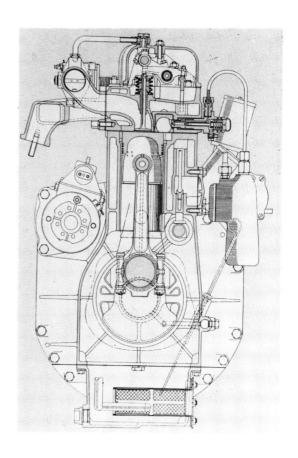

Above: The right side of the diesel engine installation. A considerable number of these tractors are still at work in 1990!

Right: The diesel engine in section showing the patented pre-combustion chamber, making it an indirect injection unit.

Below: Tractor 500000 has been preserved at the Ferguson Museum at Banner Lane, and is seen here at work in more recent times, with one of its successors, in the background.

The basic industrial tractor TEP-ZD, a petrol model with Agricultural mudguards.

A similar model with diesel engine designated TET-ZD.

A semi-industrial model was also available, this is a TET-20T Diesel model.

Above: The full industrial model featured dual brakes (hydro mechanical), fenders, bumper, grille guard and industrial tyres. Full Ferguson hydraulics were fitted and a range of approved implements and industrial equipment was available, made by outside manufacturers. The lighting equipment was designed to comply with the Road Traffic Acts.

The Last TE-20 comes off the line in 1956. This was serial number 517651, and completed the run of over half a million units in just under ten years.

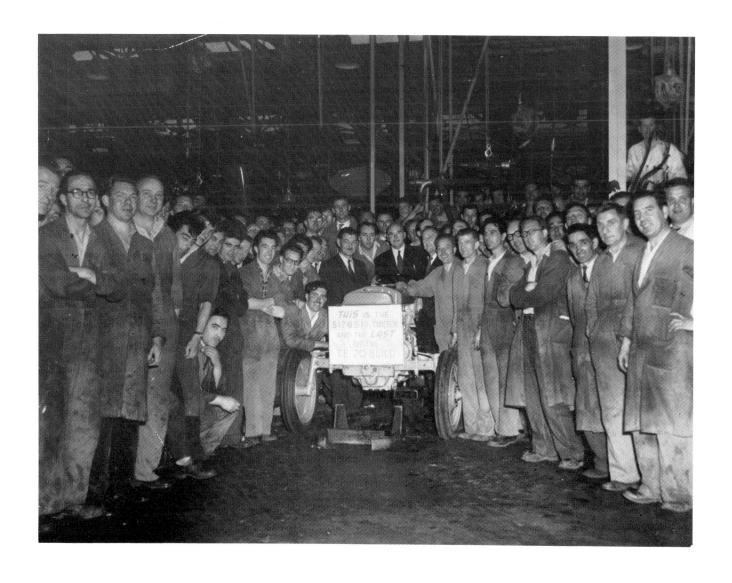

Above and left: Harry Ferguson speaking to the workforce on the occasion of the first TO-20 coming off the line at Detroit in 1948. The tractor used the same Continental Z-120 engine as was used in the UK, but note the other design differences such as the Delco Remy electrics and the foot-boards.

Top: TO-20s come off the line at the Detriot plant.

Centre: The TO-30 featured a larger engine. Here one of the first tractors comes off the line; note the badge on the bonnet which identifies this model.

Right: A TO-30 at work with a grader blade.

Left: The TO-35 retained '20' styling but in other respects it was almost identical to the British built model which took another two years to appear.

The Ferguson 40 was a 'Fergieised' Massey Harris 50 and only differed in sheet metalwork design. The tractors are seen being loaded at Ferguson's Detroit plant below.

The Ferguson 40 was introduced as an All Crop version of the TO-35. It can be seen here on the left with single front wheel, below with vee twin front wheels.

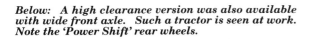

Below: A high clearance version was also available with wide front axle. Such a tractor is seen at work. Note the 'Power Shift' rear wheels.

Only the difference in tinwork identifies the Massey Harris 50 and Ferguson 40 tractors in this view outside the M-H-F factory at Detroit. Also visible are some TO-35s. The sheet metalwork of the 40 was revived on the Coventry, England built 65 when the two line range was phased out.

Centre and bottom. The MF35 as sold in the USA adopted red and metallic grey colours from 1959 and was available with Perkins diesel from the same year. We see here a Deluxe specification tractor at work and at rest, with 'Power Shift' rear wheels, extra fuel capacity, and oversize tyres.

The Massey Harris 50 was launched in 1955 to give Massey Harris dealers a Ferguson System tractor. To provide for markets in the Western Hemisphere where row-crop usage was the norm, the tractor front end was redesigned and a normal beam type axle fitted along with single drag link steering. Note also the 'Power shift' rear wheels and styling of the tinwork to accord with the then current Massey Harris range. The tractor was fitted with a Continental Z134 petrol engine, seen to the left.

The 35 was available in petrol/TVO form and the model was still available in the late fifties.

The original 35 was finished in a grey and gold livery and featured new styling. The diesel engined variant is seen right and below, and this used the Standard 23C diesel.

Above: Many readers may not realise that the predecessor of the MF65 really appeared during the War. Frank Perkins of Peterborough fitted a Ford Ferguson 9NAN with a Perkins P4 engine.

Below: The Perkins P3(TA) was adapted for use as a conversion pack for the Fergie 20. The original conversion is seen here. The engine was an Engineering dept. prototype and used standard Mark III P series parts, which included the high position water pump, large oil filter and P4 vehicle exhaust manifold.

The final version of the P3(TA) conversion pack is seen here at work. The engine developed 34BHP @ 2000rpm which was a useful increase over the normal tractor.

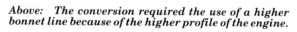

Above: The conversion required the use of a higher bonnet line because of the higher profile of the engine.

Left and Below: The installation in progress is seen here. The use of a redesigned water pump and simplified exhaust manifold lowered the bonnet line and also reduced cost!

This 35 was fitted with a Perkins P3(TA) engine for development purposes. When a Perkins engine was finally adopted, it was the P3.152 engine that was used as seen below, left and right. This development of the P3 was of 3.6" bore and 5" stroke and ran at 2200RPM to give a 33/37HP rating, and featured gear driven timing. The 35 fitted with such an engine is seen (bottom), posed at the MF training school at Stoneleigh.

Above: The 35X featured a more powerful version of the Perkins 3-152 engine, the A3-152, and was produced from 1962. Although production of the 35 ceased in the UK in 1964, assembly continued elsewhere. The shot below is most likely of a French built machine.

Above: Ferguson tractors were always popular with indus-trial and public works users. Here is a TVO 35 fitted with road tyres and fenders, and front bumper.

Below and Right: A vineyard model of the MF 35 was available with a minimum track width of 32" and overall width of 46". Fitted with 9.00 x24" rear and 5.00 x 15" rear tyres an lower profile as attained, with 10" instead of 12.25" ground clearance. A diesel model was introduced, this being the first Ferguson vineyard model to feature a c.i. engine. Note the problem of the additional batteries required for starting; these are mounted untidily on either side of the clutch housing, but are not evident on the TVO model shown to the right.

With the end of the two line policy, the Ferguson 40 and Massey Harris 50 were replaced by one model, the MF-50, seen above and below. Whilst the tractor in the top picture has the Continental Z134 engine shown on the right, the MF50 was also available with the Perkins 3.152 diesel from 1959 onwards as seen below.

Above: The IMT 539 is instantly recognisable as the MF35.
Industrija Masina Traktora of Beograd built this tractor under licence. Readers will note that a six speed gearbox was provided - "Multi-Power" was not licensed to IMT!

Below: Less recognisable but of similar ancestry is the IMT 542. Whilst this model also used the Perkins A3.152 engine, certain aspects of the transmission differed from MF standards, as a gearbox which provided 10 forward and 2 reverse gears was fitted, and this provided for four operating gears with synchromesh

One of the six LTX prototypes. In appearance it was very much a 'grown up' TE-20.

Below and below left: Some of the prototypes lasted for quite some time due to their robustness and good design.

The prototype shown here had a 4 cylinder petrol engine designated the 45C.

The 45C engined LTX with bonnet raised to show the rear mounted fuel tank. Another prototype was fitted with an L4(TA) engine from Perkins.

Above and Below: An LTX prototype was dressed up with a new bonnet to match current UK Fergie 35 styling. The view below is taken for comparison with the then current Massey Harris 50 model sold in the USA and Canada.

The MF 65 was the Massey Ferguson response to the need for a tractor in the 50HP class to compete with Ford and Nuffield. Following the realisation that the LTX prototypes would cost too much to put into production, the Western Hemisphere practice of modifying the existing model to suit was adopted. The 35 transmission was taken, and given epicyclic final reduction gearing on the outer ends of the rear axle shafts, and a Perkins 4.192 diesel was fitted. Front axle and front end were pure Ferguson 40/ Massey Harris 50, and to save on costs the press tools for the 40 tinwork, (now out of production) were shipped to the UK and the 65 given its distinctive styling. The final reduction gearing was to compensate for increase in wheel size and increased engine power; the existing gearbox being able to absorb the increased torque at higher speeds. Disc brakes were fitted, and the abandonment of the Ferguson style front axle allowed for the fitting of a single front wheel or vee twin wheels where necessary.

The UK built 65 tractors in their red and grey finish looked a deal smarter than the same styled Ferguson 40 tractors.

The MF 65 Dieselmatic sold in the USA had a different styling and the example seen here also has 'power shift' rear wheels.

Bottom: A 65, seen with matching MF trailer, is seen equipped with front wheel weights. The later Perkins AD4.203 engine developed 58.38HP @ 2000RPM.

Above; Also available were the 65R and 65S industrial models. Whilst the 65S had a normal dual clutch transmission, the 65R had an 11.75" Borg & Beck Torque Convertor and a shuttle transmission which gave four speeds in each direction. A diff. lock and handbrake were optional, as was a crankshaft hydraulic pump to operate loading shovels, etc. Power assisted steering was also available.

Below: The M-F Super 90 was only sold in the Western Hemisphere. This featured either a Continental E242 Gasoline engine or the Perkins A4-300 unit seen here. This was the first engine developed specially for tractor use by Perkins following the M-F takeover. An eight or sixteen speed shift-on-the-go transmission was employed and this model replaced the 85 which had been produced in 1958.

Above: This Fergie 20 was fitted with a Perkins 4.99 engine as the development tractor for the French built M-F 30 which can be seen below. This little tractor used the uprated version of the 4.99, the 4.107, and became the 130 in 1965. Its intention was to provide a small tractor for the French market, where many small farmers still used motor cultivators. In true French style, our example here is seen complete with fore end loader and mounted mower.

Above and below: The Tracpak was produced by a Leeds firm from early 1952 and several hundred appear to have been sold. The Sales leaflet stated that the conversion could be fitted in an hour and fifteen minutes and back to wheels in less than an hour. The illustration below shows the Perkins P3(TA) conversion to advantage.

Opposite Page: Top: This conversion was undertaken by a Mr. Burdge of Yatton, and used the tracks and sprockets from an ex army 'Weasel'. The conversion took about three hours and was designed to enable the tractor to be used as a four wheeled machine in summer and a tracked machine in winter. One problem was the steering, because the independent brakes were retained and were not really big enough for the job.

Centre: These tracks were marketed by H. Cameron Gardner Ltd., again with the quick emphasis on conversion from normal wheeled equipment.

Bottom: A 4WD conversion by Selene SAS of Italy carried out by Reekie Brothers in Scotland.

FSR 197

Seen here outside the Ferguson HQ at Fletchampstead are two of the TE-20s modified for the Antarctic expedition. On January 4th 1958 Sir Edmund Hillary reached the South Pole with 3 Ferguson petrol tractors after a three month, 1200 mile journey reaching a height of 10000 feet and in temperatures likely to reach -30 degrees F. This must have been the ultimate test for the little Fergies, which were standard models with minor modifications, e.g. heavy duty batteries, starter and wiring, plus various tracks. During the 1200 mile journey an Army 'Weasel' accompanied them but had to be abandoned after numerous breakdowns. The engines had to be adjusted to run at 3000 rpm. On reaching the South Pole, Sir Edmund Hillary arranged for a telegram to be sent to the Ferguson factory in Coventry saying how pleased he was with the tractors.

The Fergie 20 which went to the Antarctic now reposes in the Massey Ferguson Museum at Banner Lane, Coventry; for some years it was on display in one of the buildings at Stoneleigh where the museum used to be housed.

The smallest tractor in the 100 range was the French built 130. It was little different from the 825 which it replaced. It had the Perkins 4.107 engine which developed 26.96/23.06BHP, and retained the eight speed gearbox.

The 135 was the successor to the 35, using the Perkins 3.152 engine. The diesel version is seen above, whilst the Petrol engined tractor is seen below. The 135 became the 148 with the fitment of a spacer.

Above: Whilst the MF 135 built in the United Kingdom was originally turned out with a Standard 87mm engine, the majority of the petrol tractors sold were assembled in the USA, and had Continental Z-134. Later on, the petrol tractors were turned out with a new petrol engine from Perkins, the AG3.152. A small number of petrol engined demonstrators were kept in the UK for loan to Show Jumping events where they did not have the noise of the diesels to disturb the horses.

Right: The original cab fitted to the 135 was made in Glass Reinforced Plastic.

Right and below: The 135 was eventually available with the square topped fenders used on the larger models.

Left and above: late 135s had a revised front axle design, and improved engine with new type injection pump.

The 135S was designed for Industrial applications, and could be finished in an alternative yellow and grey colour scheme. The example shown is fitted with the spacer to lengthen the wheelbase.

A celebration was held to mark the 21st Anniversary of tractor production at Banner Lane. Left: Alex. Patterson, Jimmy Jones, and John Beith pose with Ferguson TE-20 number one, and in the lower shot a brand new 135, successor to the 20, is driven off the line by Works Manager Jimmy Jones.

The 165 came out originally with the old style AD4.203 engine. The updated version shown right and below which in due course became the 168 received the new version of this engine which was based on the 4.236 engine, and classified 4.212. It had the same bore as the 4.236 but a shorter stroke at 4.5"

The 165 was produced from 1965 to 1968 when it became the 168.

The 175 was the largest model to be sold in the UK. The Perkins 4.236 engine gave 63.34/55.69 BHP.

Another view of the later 175 tractor. All 100 series models sold in the UK other than the 130 were available with the usual six speed (three high/three low) transmission but the application of Multipower doubled this.

The 168 was one of the 'Super-Spec tractors added to the range in 1971. The extra features such as the spring suspension seat and gearbox spacer are clearly seen.

Not quite what it seems. Whilst the badges indicate this is a 178, the tractor is in fact equipped with a gearbox spacer which would make it a 188. Whilst the 185 nominally replaced the 178 in 1971, 178 tractors were still being built until 1972. The photograph is of one of the prototypes.

The 188 was the 'Super Spec' version of the 185. All the extras are fitted here, including PAVT rear wheels (PAVT = power assisted variable track).

Cabs are on display in these posed shots taken at Stareton.   The idea of the engine side sheets was to collect warm air from the engine and use it to heat the inside of the cab in cold weather.

The big 1100 was assembled in the USA, and was introduced in 1965. It was not sold in the UK at that time. Using the Perkins 6.354 engine, it developed into the 1130, introduced in 1966, which used a turbocharged version of the same engine.

Below: Continual development takes place with M-F products, and tractors are specially assembled for test purposes. Here is an example of such a machine involved in development work.

Above: By design or accident, Fords got lumbered with a bastard design postwar, the E27N. The Fergie 20 proved fair game for this competition, in fact the Ford salesmen dubbed it 'the grey menace'! Only half a new tractor with the familiar old Fordson engine, its ready availability and low cost made it the only real competition for the Fergie from 1946-52.

Below: Fords NAA came out of the requirement of the Ford-Ferguson Law Suit which stipulated that the 8N be withdrawn by the end of 1952. Ford launched this new model as the 'Jubilee' in 1953. It featured engine driven hydraulic pump, new OHV engine, and had position/draft control which contemporary Fergusons didn't have. This model provided the basis for all American Ford tractors until 1964, and some 250,000 were built. Over the same time Ferguson built 160,000 units at their Detroit plant.

The Competition

Other manufacturers tried to combat the success of the Ferguson tractor, especially the TE-20. Whilst it is true that the Ford 8N, whose sheer numbers in the USA eclipsed what Ferguson was able to produce, accounted for some 10 times the production of the equivalent Ferguson TO-20, in the United Kingdom the 'Grey Menace' and its sales created a thorn in the side of the other manufacturers. Fordson fought back with their Dexta, based firmly on the 9N/8N concept but with Perkins built diesel engine. International introduced the B250, the first wholly Doncaster designed project, and BMC launched their Mini Tractor, ably assisted by design staff recruited from Ferguson. Allis Chalmers tried to update their 'torque tube technology' with the D272 and ED40 models. It was just as well that the Standard tractor, born out of the loss of Banner Lane to M-F, did not materialise.

In the world of the nineteen-nineties the 'Grey Fergie' is still to be seen in number. There are many still in use on small farms and smallholdings through the length and breadth of the United Kingdom, and in many overseas territories. On the other hand, many examples are being purchased for preservation and can be seen at rallies and shows. The Ferguson 'mania' now extends to implements, and there are those who are trying to collect every variety shown in this book to attach to their 'Fergie'.

The world moves on, and agriculture must in itself prepare for the twenty first century. That need is being met by the current products of M-F, whether they be the latest 'hi-tech' models for the European arable farmer, or a basic tractor for the developing third world. It is right therefore that what can be seen coming out of Banner Lane in the 'nineties can be justly proud of its ancestry in 'The wee grey Fergie'.

Following the collapse of the Ferguson/David Brown arrangements in 1939, David Brown set about building its own tractors. Production was very restricted during the war, but the Cropmaster of 1947 was intended to be a serious competitor for the same markets as the Fergie 20. David Brown had not the production capacity to really compete, and the Cropmaster was always around £100 dearer.

International had nothing to compete with Ferguson until they launched the B250 in 1956. This tractor never gained any real inroads into the sales of 'the big two', who by this time were planning to do battle at the 'heavy' end of the scale and the 'light'.

The New Fordson Major had all that the Old one didn't and presented such a threat to Ferguson that the LTX prototypes were designed and built under the pretext of the 'big Fergie' being for export markets. In the time that Ford built the New Major in its original form, they assembled some quarter of a million units from 1952-57. In the same time Ferguson built marginally more units at 270,000. The 'big two' had the lions' share of the UK market at this time.

The biggest challenge to M-F's dominance of the 'light' end of the market came when Ford launched their 'Dexta' in 1958. Based very much on the Ford 9/8N concept this little tractor proved to be a serious competitor to the Fergie 35, and had one advantage that the engine was a good starter. In the years 1957-60 Fordson went to the top of the sales table in the UK, despite the launch of the MF 65.

The Dexta had a six year run from 1958-64 during which it was continually improved and a more powerful model, the Super Dexta introduced. Strange to say, most of the engines for this tractor were built and supplied whilst Perkins was under M-F control! Shown here is a post 1960 standard model.

Like MF, Ford consolidated its range worldwide in 1964/5 and here is an example of the competition which MF faced from Ford in the mid sixties. The 3000 was the second in a new range of of four models. Strange to say, the MF 100 range also featured the same number of options.

While Fordson concentrated on the 'heavy' end of the market, other manufacturers had sights on pecking away at the 'light' end, and Nuffield launched its 'Universal Three' in August 1957, just ahead of Fordson moving into the 'light' end as well. It was very much a scaled down 'Universal Four' using many common parts. Ford decided not to take the same approach when they moved in this direction.

Allis Chalmers always played with the 'light' end of the market with a succession of models assembled at Totton near Southampton based on the original US built model B. These, from 1948 ran through the EB, D270, and D272 models, culminating in the ED40 launched in 1958, which used the Standard 23C engine. The Standard Motor Co. had a surplus of these units when M-F went Perkins. Numbers sold of all models were never a serious threat to Ferguson. Who would buy a 'B' when you could have a solid little 'Fergie' for around the same price in 1950?

The launch of the BMC 'Mini Tractor' in 1965 saw a tractor based very much on 'Fergie' principles. It was no coincidence that one of the chief designers was recruited from M-F, and that all the testing work was done by Harry Ferguson (Research) Ltd., a company set up by HF which was totally independant of Massey Ferguson. The 948cc diesel was developed from the proven BMC 'A' series engine of the Mini, but the early examples were gutless wonders. The result was the 1968 launch of the Nuffield 4/25 which had a 1.5 litre engine (below).

FERGUSON MODEL DESIGNATIONS

Type A.	David Brown built tractors 1936-7.
9N	Fo'rd built tractors 1939-41
9NAN	Fo'rd built tractors with V.O engine for U.K. 1939-41
2N	Fo'rd built utility model 1942-45
2NAN	Fo'rd built utility model with V.O engine for U.K. 1942-45
TE-20	Standard built tractor with Continental Z-120 engine, 1946-48 (1)
TEA-20	Standard built tractor with Standard engine, petrol. 1947-56 (2) (3).
TO-20	Detroit built tractor with Continental Z-120 engine 1948-31 (1)
TEB-20	Standard built tractor with Continental engine, narrow, 1946-48 (1)
TEC-20	Standard built tractor with Standard engine, narrow, 1948-56 (2) (3).
TED-20	Standard built tractor with V.O. Standard engine, 1949-56 (2) (3).
TEE-20	Standard built tractor with V. O. Standard engine, narrow, 1949-56 (2) (3).
TEF-20	Standard built tractor with Standard diesel engine 1951-56 (6).
TO-30	Detroit built tractor with Continental Z-129 engine, 1951-54 (4)
TEH-20	Standard built tractor with Standard Zero Octane engine 1950-56 (2) (3)
TEJ-20	Standard built tractor with Standard Z.O. engine, narrow, 1950-56, (2) (3).
TEK-20	Standard built tractor with Standard Petrol engine, Vineyard, 1952-56 (3).
TEL-20	Standard built tractor with Standard Z.O. engine, Vineyard, 1952-56 (3)
TEM-20	Standard built tractor with Standard Z.O. engine, Vineyard, 1952-56 (3)
TEP-20	Standard built tractor with Standard Petrol engine, Industrial, 1952-56 (3)
TER-20	Standard built tractor with Standard V.O. engine, Industrial, 1952-56 (3)
TES-20	Standard built tractor with Standard Z.O. engine, Industrial, 1952-56 (3)
TET-20	Standard built tractor with Standard Diesel engine, Industrial 1952-56 (6)
TO-35	Detroit built tractor with Continental Z-134 engine, 1954-57. (5)
FE-40	Detroit built tractor with Continental Z-134 engine, 1956-57. (5) Ferguson
MH-50	Detroit built tractor with Continental Z-134 engine, 1955-58 (5) Massey.
FE-35	Standard built tractor with Standard engine 1956-58.
MF-35	Standard/ MF built tractor with Standard engine 1958-59
MF-35	MF built tractor with Perkins 3.152 engine 1959-62.
MF-35X	MF built tractor with Perkins A3-152 engine 1962-64.
MF-65	MF built tractor with Perkins 4.192 engine 1958-60
MF-65MkII	MF built tractor with Perkins AD4.203 engine 1958-65.
MF-25	MF French built tractor with Perkins 4.107 engine 1963-65.
MF-88	MF Detriot built tractor with Continental Diesel 1960-1962.
MF Super 90.	MF Detriot built tractor with Perkins A4.300 engine 1961-1965.
MF-130	MF French built tractor with Perkins 4.107 engine, 1966-72
MF-135	MF built tractor with Perkins A3.152/ Continental Z145/ Perkins AG3.152 engine 1965-79.
MF-148	MF built tractor with Perkins A3.152 engine 1972-1979
MF-150	MF Detroit built tractor with engines as MF-135. 1965-75
MF-165	MF built tractor with Perkins AD4.203 engine 1965-68.
MF-168	MF built tractor with Perkins A4.212 engine 1968-1979.
MF-175	MF built tractor with Perkins A4.236 engine 1971-1979.
MF-178	MF built tractor with Perkins A4.236 engine 1965-1968
MF-185	MF Detriot built tractor with Perkins A4.236 engine 1965-74.
MF-188	MF built tractor with Perkins A4.248 engine 1968-1971
MF-1100	MF built tractor with Perkins A4.248 engine 1971-1979
MF-1130	MF built tractor with Perkins A4.248 engine 1971-1979
MF-1200	MF Detriot built tractor with Perkins A6.354 engine 1965-72.
MF-1080	MF Detriot built tractor with Perkins A6.354 engine 1965-72
MF-1200	MF built tractor with Perkins AT6.354 engine 1965-72
MF-1130	MF built tractor with Perkins A6.334 engine 1972-79
MF-1080	MF built tractor with Perkins A4.318 engine 1969-75

Ferguson and Massey Ferguson Tractors. Engine Specifications.

Make	Cyls.	Bore x Stroke	CC.	Fuel	HP	Used in.
C. Climax/D.B.	4	3.125" x 4"	2010	G/K	20	Type 'A'
Ford	4	3.187" x 3.75"	1966	G/K	23.87	9N/2N/9NAN.
Cont. Z-120	4	81mm x 95mm	1966	G.	23.9	TE-20/TO-20(1)
Standard	4	80mm x 92mm	1850	G. G/K	23.9	TEA-20 etc.(2)
Standard	4	85mm x 92mm	2088	G. G/K	28.2	TEA-20 etc.(3)
Cont. Z-129	4	3.25" x 3.875"	2113	G.	30.27	TO-30 (4)
Cont. Z-134	4	3.3125" x 3.875"	2195	G.	32.80	TO-35, F-40, (5)
Standard	4	80.96mm x101.6mm	2092	D.	26.00	TEF-20 (6)
Perkins P3(TA)	3	3.5" x 5"	2360	D.	34.00	Conversion pack.
Perkins P6(TA)	6	3.5" x 5"	4730	D.	46.00	MH 744.
Perkins L4(TA)	4	4.25 x 4.75"	4420	D.	50.00	MH 745
Standard	4	87mm x 92mm	2186	G. G/K	34.00	FE 35, 135 Petrol.
Standard 23C	4	84.14 x 101.6mm	2258	D.	34.00	FE 35,
Perkins 4.192	4	3.6" x 5".	3335	D.	55.50	MF 65MkI
Perkins 3.152	3	3.6" x 5".	2489	D.	35.00	MF 35, MF 50.
Perkins A3-152	3	3.6" x 5"	2500	D.	41.50	MF 35X, MF 50, MF 135
Perkins AD4-203	4	3.6 x 5"	3335	D.	55.50	MF 65Mk II. MF 165.
Cont. G 176	4	3.58" x 4.38"	2883	G	46.92	MF 65. (W.H.) MF 165
Cont. Z 145	4	3.375" x 4.062"	2376	G	35.36	MF 135 D/L, MF 150
Perkins AG3.152	3	3.6" x 5"	2489	G	35.00	Late MF 135/ MF 150.
Perkins AG4.212	4	3.875" x 4.5"	3472	G	55.00	MF 165.
Perkins A4.212	4	3.875" x 4.5"	3472	D	58.30	late MF 165.
Perkins A4.236	4	3.875" x 5"	3865	D	63.34	MF 175/168.
Perkins A4.248	4	3.980" x 5"	4062	D.	68.00	MF 178/185/188
Perkins A4.300	4	4.5" x 4.75"	4950	D.	68.00	MF Super 90.
Cont. G 206	4	3.9" x 4.5"	3374	G.	62.33	MF 175, MF 180
Perkins AG4.236	4	3.875" x 5"	3865	G.	62.00	MF 175, MF 180
Perkins 4.107	4	3.125" x 3.5"	1752	D.	26.96	MF 825, MF130.
Perkins A6.354	6	3.875" x 5"	5798	D.	93.94	MF1100
Perkins AT6.354	6	3.875" x 5"	5798	TD.	120.51	MF1130
Perkins A4.318	4	4.5" x 5"	3185	D	81.96	MF1080
Waukesha F320-G	6	4.125" x 4"	5341	G.	90.29	MF1100

Notes: G=Gasoline. G/K= Petrol/TVO. D=Diesel. TD=Turbocharged Diesel. The numbers in brackets ( ) refer to the list of model codes below.

N.B. Most 100 series tractors sold in the Western Hemisphere were also available with gasoline engines. See engine specification table for details.

SERIAL NUMBERS

Unless indicated, the first serial number in each year is shown.

Ferguson Black Prototype Tractor.
1 only produced 1933.

Ferguson Model 'A' made by David Brown Tractors.
1250 made between 1936 and 1938
1-550 Coventry Climax engine.
551-1350 David Brown engine.

Ford 9N/9NAN/2N/2NAN. with Ferguson System Built Dearborn.

1939 (July)	1	1943	107755
1940	14644	1944	131783
1941	47843	1945	174638
1942	92363	1946	204129
		1947	267289
		end	306221

Ferguson TE 20 model made by Standard Motor Company.

1946	1	1952	241336
1947	315	1953	310780
1948	20895	1954	367999
1949	77773	1955	428093
1950	116462	1956	488579
1951	167837	end	517651

First Standard engine used September 1947.
TE (Continental) and TEA (Standard) engined tractors were built side by side up to serial 48000.
Last Continental engine used July 1948.
First TED (VO) model built April 1949.
85mm engine (Petrol and TVO) cut in at Serial No. 172501 on 22.1.51.
First TEF (Diesel) model built January 1951.
12 Volt Electrics phased in from Serial 250001

Ferguson 35/ Massey Ferguson 35 built at Coventry.

1956	1001	1961	220614
1957	9226	1962	267528
1958	79553	1963	307231
1959	125068	1964	352255
1960	171471	end	388382

First FE35 built October 1956.
First MF35 (Red/Grey) built November 1957
Last Standard 23c engine 166595.
First Perkins 3-152 engine 166596 (November 1959).
MF35X introduced December 1962 (with Multipower).

Massey Ferguson 65 Built at Coventry.

1958	500001	1962	551733
1959	510451	1963	552325
1960	520569	1964	593028
1961	533180	end	614024

First MF65 Mark I built December 1957.
First MF65 Mark II introduced November 1960
First A4-203 engine 531453.
Multipower Introduced August 1962.

Ferguson TO20/ TO30 Built by Harry Ferguson Inc. Detriot.

1948 (Oct)	1	1952	72680
1949	1808	1953	108645
1950	14660	1954	125959
1951	39163	end	140000

TO-30 cut in at Serial No. 60001 in August 1951.

Ferguson TO-35 Built by Massey Harris Ferguson Inc. Detroit.

1954	140001	1956	167157
1955	140006	1957	171741

TO-35 Gas Deluxe.

1958	178216	1960	203680
1959	188851	1961	207427

TO-35 Gas Special.

1958	183348	1960	203198
1959	185504	1961	209484

TO-35 Diesel

1958	180742	1960	203360
1959	187719	1961	203680

Ferguson 40 Built by Massey Harris Ferguson Inc. Detroit.

1956	400001	1957	405671

Massey Harris 50 Built by Massey Harris Ferguson Inc. Detroit.

1955	500001	1957	510764
1956	500473	1958	515708

Following the cessation of the two line policy (F-40 and MH-50 tractors were assembled on the same production line), the model became the MF-50.

Massey Ferguson 135.

1965	101	1969	117429
1966	30283	1970	141426
1967	67597	1971	162200
1968	93305		

Massey Ferguson 135 updated.

1971	400001	1976	457866
1972	403518	1977	469335
1973	419583	1978	479192
1974	432709	1979	487350
1975	445602	end	490714

Massey Ferguson 165.

1965	500001	1969	563701
1966	512207	1970	581457
1967	530825	1971	597745
1968	547384		

Massey Ferguson 165 updated.

1971	100001	1976	145432
1972	103622	1977	155687
1973	116353	1978	164417
1974	126448	1979	173144
1975	135036	end	173696

Massey Ferguson 175 (178 from 1968)

1965	700001	1969	732158
1966	705652	1970	740301
1967	714166	1971	747283
1968	722679	1972	753108

Massey Ferguson 175 S

1968	650000	1971	656011
1969	652061	1972	657362
1970	653721		

Massey Ferguson 148

1972	600001	1977	609159
1973	602153	1978	609969
1974	604449	1979	610893
1975	605578	end	610982
1976	607701		

Massey Ferguson 168

1971	250001	1976	258064
1972	250005	1977	259959
1973	252121	1978	260617
1974	254307	1979	261103
1975	255967	end	261173

Massey Ferguson 185

1971	300001	1976	326109
1972	302833	1977	332107
1973	310398	1978	335211
1974	315219	1979	339755
1975	319923	end	340096

Massey Ferguson 188

1971	350001	1976	365087
1972	350006	1977	368350
1973	353296	1978	370156
1974	357063	1979	371306
1975	360784	end	371333

ISBN
1 85638 029 7

VINTAGE TRACTOR & MACHINERY PUBLICATIONS
£9.50